The
Backwaters
Press

The BACKWATERS
PRIZE IN POETRY
Honorable Mention

EVERYBODY'S JONESIN' *for* SOMETHING

INDIGO MOOR

The Backwaters Press · An imprint of the University of Nebraska Press

Acknowledgments for the use of copyrighted
material appear on page ix, which constitutes
an extension of the copyright page.

Library of Congress
Cataloging-in-Publication Data
Names: Moor, Indigo, author.
Title: Everybody's jonesin' for
something / Indigo Moor.
Description: Lincoln: The Backwaters Press,
an imprint of the University of Nebraska
Press, [2021] | Series: The Backwaters
Prize in Poetry Honorable Mention
Identifiers: LCCN 2020039755
ISBN 9781496222701 (paperback)
ISBN 9781496225306 (epub)
ISBN 9781496225313 (mobi)
ISBN 9781496225320 (pdf)
Subjects: LCGFT: Poetry.
Classification: LCC PS3613.O5535
E94 2021 | DDC 811/.6—dc23
LC record available at
https://lccn.loc.gov/2020039755

Set and designed in Questa by N. Putens.

For
J.T., J.G., and I.M.
It's been a long road.

Jonesin'

1. **SURFACE:** *craving, wanting*
   Usage: "Man, I am jonesin' for a hamburger."

2. **DEEPER:** *an ache we, in turn, ache to scratch*
   Usage: "Even my dreams are jonesin' for her voice; it wakes me up."

3. **DEEPER STILL:** *an ache we punish others, often incorrectly, for forcing us to face*
   Usage: "There is a land, a forgiveness, a perfection our ancestors knew, and I am jonesin' to see it manifest, here, under my feet."

4. **DEEPEST:** *a cannibalistic drive that devours your existence and transforms your being until it becomes your heart*
   Usage: "I'm jonesin'. God help me, I'm jonesin' . . ."

CONTENTS

We the *(Chameleon)* People

ACKNOWLEDGMENTS

The poems below first appeared in the following publications:

Banyan Review: "Veterans of Foreign Wars," "American Bataan,"
    "Finder of Lost Sheep"
Brilliant Corners: "All Night," "Jazz," "From the Sisyphus Club"
Marsh Hawk Review: "Lost in the World Machine"
Stonecoast Review: "Catching a Cotton Ball"
Tule Review: "Unjumping the Broom," "Christ Is Summoned to the
    House of the Broken Ladder"

California Fire & Water: A Climate Crisis Anthology, ed. Molly Fisk
    (Story Street Press, 2020)
      "The Party Crashers of Paradise"
Fragments, with Barry Ebner (Berkeley: The Studio of Nothing Else, 2018)
    "Frac/Tured"

In the private collection of Danyen Powell
    "Exiled to America"

EVERYBODY'S JONESIN' FOR SOMETHING

This American Groove

Love Letter to Dr. Ford from the Patriarchy

Dear Christine:

What has happened
      to our women?   I won't drag
reason into your delusion,
swatting
     at windmills
        with a broom.

You complain even as a thousand cameras
      section you like a hog:
In the fifties,
       we would've doused
       your furnace
with Valium.

My mother   could watch
       hummingbirds for hours.
The inside of her skull
     Rorschach flashcards.

But the pot roast was never late.

Honey, I'm fighting
     for this country.

Cracking eagle eggs
      into frying pans
            to make us great again.
Rebranding swastikas;
      painting the arms
red-striped and blue-eyed.

Hell, I'll reach my hand   up Lady Liberty's
            copper skirt
      and goose the flame, if I have to.

Sluice purple mountains.
      Pan the American dream
      from streams crimson
            with Native American tears.
And this is how you thank
            the architects of Paradise.

Be reasonable.   Drag the viper
      from the cigar box.
Patriotism is a horse
      losing your name in a bet.

Open this gift box.
      Here's a charred chunk
            of Greenwood.
Some faded California Camp pictures:
      Remember how we tossed
peanuts at Japs in cages
            until laughter carved
stitches in our kidneys?

Slow your heart.
        Guzzle this Librium martini.
Let's fold the top down,
            ride through the sunset
                    like Roy and Dale.

We'll pitch tents in the Alamo.
        My guitar strung
with real Mexican guts.

I'm building two McDonald's
        for every crack
in the Wall.   Christ, woman,
                have you ever felt safer?

Take this Prozac Lemon Drop
            and voting sheet
        already filled out for you.

Christen my yacht.
        We'll save money
on fireworks:
            shoot immigrants
from cannons on the fourth.

Finish the dishes.
        We'll have sex
            on the foreclosure papers
        that turn Harlem
into a street mall.

It won't be college-

                        fucking

But is it ever?

Hush, Chrissie.

Maybe you were assaulted.
           But,
      Bet dollars to doughnuts,
you enjoyed it.

Trayvon Martin Disappears on Stage

The Shooter said that Trayvon Martin Went for His Gun

THE RED CROW, THE MAN ON TOP.

He was first   an afterthought:
There was once flesh
                        in that hole,
smoking like a highway-broke Chevy.

Downtown:
        A bartender cradles
                    a cigar wreath
as the TV news bleats the scene
        like a huddled mass of sheep.
He is late for home.
        His wife slumps
the edge of their bed   filing
        her nails   the lost years.

He knows the unwalked dog has pissed
                the floor.   But the cigar
        is so   damn RIGHT
                scissored between
                        first and second fingers.
The last puff exhales coppery.

        He focuses back center stage.
                The black villain's punctured lung
                        is filled with (not his,
                                by Christ) cold blood.

THE WHITE HAT, THE BOY ON TOP.

Tray-something was on top
                punching MMA style.
His hoodie   sheltering
      a constellation
               of black stars,   black
                      wholes & halves.
The cotton string
      tugs a legion of necks
            stretched
      to some other quadrant of universe.

An old woman walks
      a pinch-tailed dog,
twitching   whining
for an unmarked fire hydrant
               that never comes.

When the metallic *pop*
      stings air like a jab
the Boy's head opens
             like a door
meant only to be closed.

There's a mote
      in both his eyes
          no God recognizes.

THE BLUE TREE, THE INVISIBLE ROPE.

This neighborhood is riddled,
      black   jack   hornets

strafing sidewalks
        like acid raindrops.

You can't call it   *race*
    when one group runs,
        the other   bolted
to a crawl   starter pistol
    crushed against their temple.

This is what we know:
        a large *Man*
    unwrapped a gun
from a wooden box.

The *Boy* is shot.

Elsewhere
A farmer   leans on a scythe
        like a rake,
    recounting the scene
        to his wife

    as a prism   a snow globe
    a black kite plunging   a foxhole

        The foxhole where their son   died
            screaming
            his parent's name.

Back center scene
a police cruiser straddles
    the reclaimed block
like a hen guarding an egg.

There is a crowd
    There are a dozen
        Empty-pocketed gazes.

    There's a bible.
        There's a noose.
            There's a flag.

The New Math

2016. Holocaust: the year the president declared war on colors and poverty. We know every crack in the mortar, where the House crumbles beneath its own weight and circumstance.	6. A fact is a phrase that tells half a story to some, closes a country's eyes. *See* immigrant policy. *See* Dream trapped in its own hourglass.
3. River Crossing: a place where you drain the water and bury sanity in the soft mud. Keep speaking to me of the borders we keep in mind.	45. The carcass of the Constitution, bloated goat on White House stairs. Several laws crisscross a stale river.
2&Rising. Hijab: covering snatched before pushing Muslim down stairs. *See* child hovering On the leading edge of a : sine wave : Hate *you*	Unknown #. Woman: a thing you pave the streets with. *See* BLACK. My alter ego is a man walking backward in time.
500 bullets. 1 Gun. If it is raining glassy tears, the country is safe . . . Yes. Great Again.	1. Name for Mother. Never two, unless it's chosen, *chosen*, choice, choose, chance, love
1. Name for Father. Never two, unless it's chosen, *chosen*, choice, choose, chance, love	Zero: days the country is assault free. The television laughs like a wildfire hose.
You are not the case, the note tuned an octave up. Crane, an animal balanced on one rule of law. Rushed, backlogged, how many ways is *No* said. Ah, how is it always not about money today?	2020: *See* Cliff, *See* Tight Rope. *See* rope. *See* gun. *See* Fire This Time. *See* Next Time. *See* other side of Country. To be continued.

Extinction Event

My grandmother would kneel before me, stick one finger inside the starched collar of my dress shirt, and pull me to her. With a firm grip on the knot of my clip-on tie, her knuckle on my Adam's apple, she slathered Vaseline on my face, careful to smooth out all the rough spots. I always pulled back, forcing her to say, *hold still, boy,* as if I didn't know what I was supposed to be doing. It's hard to say why I struggled. Maybe because I was seven. Maybe because the shirt was for a six-year-old version of me and, even without her finger inside, the collar felt like two hundred years of black, Southern Jesus trying to strangle me.

Mostly, I think I resisted because of my reaction to the library that opened near our house.

The first book I checked out was a giant book called *Dinosaurs: A to Z.* Twenty pages with full-color illustrations. Apparently, the most important part about dinosaurs is that they died, because that is how the book began. The author speculated that a few million years ago, something came from the sky, crashed into the earth, and killed them off. Like most tough, quasi-country boys, I secretly slept with both feet under the covers, afraid of what might wake at night and reach for me. Now, I was also afraid of what might come from the sky when I closed my eyes.

Apparently, the destruction of the dinosaurs did not happen quickly. At least not to the dinosaurs far away from ground zero. Like me, they had time to pull away, thinking, *No, I don't understand this. No, this feels wrong. And, if it must happen, can somebody tell me why?* But meteors don't explain themselves any more than grandparents. Meteors hit the planet. Dinosaurs die. They spend millions of years digesting inside the bowels of the planet. Then they get sucked up, mixed with a bunch of other stuff, and smeared across the faces of little black boys.

With that much misery spread on my face each week to meet Jesus, is it any wonder I drifted from the church? Okay, that's not fair. There are at least a dozen reasons I wasn't suited for Christianity. And while dinosaurs on my face wasn't reason number one, it certainly wasn't close to number twelve. I was a sensitive boy who had no words to express myself. Mostly when faced with uncertainty, I set my teeth, closed my mouth, and squirmed. I don't know how many dinosaurs came to church on my face over the years, but there had to have been hundreds. I imagined triceratopses because they were my favorites. Brontosauruses because just one of them could flatten the church with a swing of its tail. And, of course, Tyrannosaurus Rexes because, hey, why not the entire congregation running screaming while I snuck off to the store with my tithe money. But, after all the imagined carnage ran through my head, all that was left were dinosaur hostages, like me, all trapped on a church pew. All of them scared, lonely, and bewildered, mouthing along to words that *almost* made sense. Rituals that *almost* came together in their heads.

Why did I answer the preacher's call to *Come to Jesus* and be baptized? I did it because I hoped it would make my grandmother happy. My family was sewn into the church, my grandfather's name engraved on the plaque hammered at eye-level into bricks by the entrance. As for me. What can I say? I wasn't feeling Jesus. I read the Bible because the stories were pretty cool. Looking back, I can see how that gave people the wrong impression. My family hoped I would grow up to be a preacher. I imagined I would grow up to rewrite the stories. Maybe get one of the Books named after me. Let's face it: some of them go on forever, and you can see the endings coming a mile away. Children are hyperaware of not fitting in, of being a disappointment. But, if the stories were to be believed, I could remove my sin with a quick dip in a pool.

When you are an overimaginative boy, very few ideas survive the first implementation. I admit the pomp and circumstance of the moment got to me. By the time Reverend Wallace was ready to dunk me into the water, I was so wound up and nervous, there was no way the altercation would not end in a fight. When he grabbed me by the back of the neck and my shoulders to lower me into the concrete pool beneath the pulpit, I fought back. But he was bigger and more practiced. In the end, he subdued me and held me under. Water shot up my nose. I coughed. Somebody, hazy through the shimmering, yelled, *Praise Jesus!*

My baptism only delayed the inevitable. The day I told my grandmother I didn't want to go to church anymore, all she said was okay. She didn't argue. She didn't try to convince me. Everyone else got dressed and left for the service. I stayed in my pajamas and watched cartoons.

Things were never the same between my grandparents and me. Every Sunday, the gulf widened. Once, fed up with my obstinance, my grandfather said, "That boy needs to be baptized."

My grandmother sniffed behind the mesh veil of one of her more sparkly church hats. "He got baptized last year." They were speaking loudly. They wanted me to hear.

My grandfather laughed. "Maybe he should go back and try again."

After they left, I turned off the TV and went back to bed.

Dinosaurs A to Z was adamant in its conclusion. Some dinosaurs must have survived that historic meteor strike. They woke up the next day to fires, debris, and ash. They picked themselves up and went on living their lives, knowing they couldn't undo what had happened. And, even if they could, they wouldn't know where to start.

All Night . . .

We're in L.A., twitterpated
when the last wall
    crashes down like Jericho
    and we are irrevocably
    in love. I'm sorry for that.
    When I saw you standing

the platform—
A noir film star
    hitting all your marks
    blocking ground light
    like every Norse god
    sewn to a silhouette—

I should have tilted
my hat, slunk into
    my seat and rolled by.
    Honey, you and I
    are bad news. A headline
    that won't stop repeating

the word **TRAINWRECK**.
What we do to each other
    is animal. Pan tilts his horns
    to jitterbugging sheets.
    Sheepish, honeycombed grin
    melting through our blinds.

We're buck-toothed
hungry for the stuttering
    love-thing we become.
    Two drunks. No pretense
    at lucidity. No reason
    to sober up. What can I say?

Our bodies fit.
Constellations
    pulsing stone-sweet angst.
    There's no sunshine
    to this flesh song
    of ours, devouring:

We crave

    So we crave

Then crave some more.

. . . Jazz . . .

We're StreetSide,
your suitcase wrestling
over drowned pleas.
This is how the heart
turns on you: the weight
of broken vows cracks

the walls, our throats
swell like a sunbaked
highway. I'm sycophant
to your grace. The devil
in your eyes can break
necks, quell storms.

Can truth plague a man's
head to his chest plate?
We could try again, but
there's no reason, no
end to some struggles.
Platitudes hum a weak

Glissando. One more
loopy try might split
flesh-crossed sutures;
pawprints breaking
into whistling song. The taxi's
headlights are never soon

Enough. Shadows mimicking
bellboys, shimmy suitcases
into the cave maw of the trunk.
Lord, grant me this prayer:
don't let her eyes target my tears.
But who is this tin man without a heart?

Fuck it. Honey, come on
back. Let's drag another
tune from Sisyphus. Until
our lips splinter and crack
against the reed. Until the drunken
sunset staggers over the horizon.

. . . from the Sisyphus Club

I've wrapped
two peacocks
in silk and hit
the trainyard, betting
all-night hoboing
will melt you

into my arms.
The conductor's lazy
eye is stuck skyward
transfixed
to the super moon
blood-orange plopped

in the night stir of bitters
and stars. I'm curled up,
pill-bugged into a steamer
car. Moonlight frisbees
off my back, puddles
in the corner, vibrating

off wicked dust.

In thirty minutes
I'll steal up the ladder
to your room,
    silent as a wave
    shaking wind off

    its back, whispering
    something sweet &
wintry into your ear.
It'll goose-walk down
    to your dreams. Plant
    a blood rose in your hands

like a flag
like a vow.
    Know this:
    the salt-kiss
from my lips
stains every petal.

    By the time you wake,
    I'm back on the train
your smile tucked in my coat.

Creole Rumspringa

I never thanked you   for your Black Heart   For bucking your paper bag
friends For bumping thighs to Sugar Hill   The funk I gave, and you took   For the
two-by-two of four-by-fours   Forgive my blackness stain on your high yellow
dinner table Thank you for slipping me the right fork for the salad When the crow swooped,
your daddy drew a lead hole through its heart   then looked at me like a wish he
forgot to make   Remember that   Your hallway to five bedrooms for three people   DAMN
That's still dizzying   A solid oak room waiting to be filled   A vacuum for unwritten
laughter   Sorry I wore tattered dress converse to your party   Your mother's unbroken
rhythm of *tsks* and condescension still rankles my ass   Your uncle asked where
my father went to school   My teeth ground unspun glass   *Incog-negro*: I get the
joke now   You called me Invisible Man   I thought Claude Rains   I never dreamed
you'd want to slap   the country grin   out my mouth   strain out my   black & ugly.

The Fortress of First and Last Thoughts

I'm reading Kaminski, deaf to the war of clinking glasses and forks when she slides into her chair, trailing grace like a vapor trail, her fingernails the color of smoldering ashes. She taps the table's edge, a writer's gong to begin a new litany:

What she says:
Her new manuscript languished beside the cat food on her kitchen counter, simultaneously undone and somehow sadly finished She saw Harriet Tubman in a theatre with no color but her own She lost her husband last week and was considering taking out a restraining order He simply would not leave her thoughts her heart her moments The roasted peppers sprinkled with Himalayan salt were new and simply divine.

The waiter arrives and suggests a sauvignon blanc neither of us has a story about. Intolerable for a writer such as me.

What I say:
My latest manuscript took second place in a major contest and will arrive before spring breaks ice in the next year Three old shirts of mine were resurrected by circular styling A stroke days before Christmas almost stole half of my body my senses my speech For a day I was a cliff pulled half into sea by a storm The latest additions to my memoir make me wonder if I know myself I already despair duplicating this divine pepper recipe at home.

The meal ends with a grapefruit salad and a kiss that tastes vaguely of stale air. Later, the phone wakes me from a quasi-slumber dream of moonlight pounding a Moroccan beach. She wants to know what I said earlier that reminded her of the Italian roadster her husband flew over a cliff in Big Sur, pistons flailing like broken wings. But the only memory I have of dinner is of a ghost frantically dialing a number no one answers.

Christh Is Summoned to the House
of the Broken Ladder

Bless   this old poet
head fractured,
rung like a bell
tied at the edge
of a deep forest.

Bless   the rotted wood
the splintered perch.

Bless   the skull blood
the oil stain
the missing shoe
cradled like love
in a stray dog's teeth.

Bless   the silence.

Bless   the unwashed window's
feeble gleam;

A bevy of ghosts
traipse across the pane.

Bless   the patio table's groan
swaybacked, weighed
under a hideous load:
a single plate
a single ache
a single glass.

Bless   the single glass
bless the loneliness.

Bless   the unhinged knee
the bruised flesh
swelling like scarred bread.

Now,   Poet   Rise.
I unhinge the darkness
webbed into your brain
like a backward dream,

I rehang your crooked life
on its damaged hook. But
for my name taken in vain
as you pinwheeled through
dusk like a broken doll

I leave you all the sadness.

Mamie Till & the Minotaur

For my Sister, Erika

She pounces the Minotaur's crumbling trail
as Emmett's wail retreats on a moon-drenched tide.
Has there ever been light in this drizzled air
hanging like bushmasters from stone precipices?
Secrets punch the gloaming like shotgun blasts.

She turns left, then right, past Bobo's head
carved on a riverbed like a flimsy excuse.
A rusty fan somersaults the Tallahatchie breeze.
Every hill croons birthright and privilege, stripped
down answers to questions no one ever asks.

If she could call back her child, the whole damn
South might lose weight, fall knee-deep into shame.

I don't know if this part is myth or not:
She rounds a corner to the Minotaur corralled
by a lie. From a pocket, she drags the only
thing this beast fears: an open casket.

What Was True and Not So. And Yet, Again . . .

He   (let's call him Ralph)   wakes up driving a highway.   Headlights

splatter against a wall of damp fog.   What's in his head?   He stands on the brakes

stupefied.   And mewls.   A dog steel-toed by a cruel master.   **END STORY.**

PROLOGUE: He is a man without a name: Let's call all his love   Unrequited

He's wholesome as a spit-shine.   His camos   starched   & sacred.   Think red lipstick

on a whore.   He always thought he had a horseshoe for a soul.   His gun hand

His handgun   hand   carved into a gun   shakes in a wind-swept Dixie breeze.

He's at a black church.   No, a gay club.   A rooftop.   A *somewhere* lost to him.

The fog: You can be anyone behind a white cloak: A doctor with a cure

for a sick country   A savior.   A white hat   A martyr   on a fog-stenched path.

Clandestine redemption.   A   bloodletting.   An **EPILOGUE.**   God Bless . . .

Unforgettable

DAUGHTER is asleep. MOTHER walks in and begins PLAYING A LULLABY. PHONE RINGS. MOTHER stops and scurries back as DAUGHTER awakes. DAUGHTER looks at the number, then answers.

DAUGHTER

Hello? Yeah, I took the room phone off the hook. A package. How big? Okay. Give me thirty minutes and bring it up to my room.

DAUGHTER hangs up the phone and attempts to go back to sleep. MOTHER moves closer, preparing to play again. PHONE RINGS. MOTHER looks at the number. MOTHER gently shakes DAUGHTER then scurries back. DAUGHTER answers the phone.

DAUGHTER

Hey, Dad, No, I'm up. I don't have time to talk. I got an interview with a radio station in an hour. I'll be playing my new alto on air. Just picking out my clothes.

MOTHER picks through the closet, selecting clothes to suggest to DAUGHTER.

DAUGHTER (CONT.)

Yeah, it does matter. Cause there's always a photoshoot. I made that mistake on my first tour. Showed up at a radio station in Queens looking all . . . No, I was not going to say "ghetto." And not "country." Let's not start that. Dad. Dad. If I was ashamed of where I came from, how come I'm back in Shreveport right now? I was gon' call. I just got in last night.

DAUGHTER stands and begins looking through clothes,
ignoring MOTHER. MOTHER gives up and sits on the
bed, holding saxophone.

DAUGHTER (CONT.)

Can we talk after the interview? I really need to get ready. You got the tickets I sent? You can ask Momma if you want to. I can't wait to hear her response.

(*Exasperated*)

What's her excuse this time?

MOTHER reacts to the news she knows her DAUGHTER
is hearing. MOTHER stands and approaches audience
as DAUGHTER sits on bed.

MOTHER

A jazz player that can't use silence doesn't know how to play. You can make some notes better by getting rid of the noise of other notes.

MOTHER PLAYS A FRENETIC tune as DAUGHTER
absorbs the news. MUSIC stops. MOTHER sits beside
DAUGHTER on the bed. MOTHER wants to touch
DAUGHTER, but she does not quite touch her.

DAUGHTER

I heard she was sick, but that was a while back. I didn't know. Daddy, her and I haven't talked in years.

DAUGHTER rises, pacing, agitated. MOTHER walks to
front of stage, facing crowd, absorbing all that is said
about her, reacting.

DAUGHTER (CONT.)

Don't put this on me. I'm not that hard to reach. It's not like I roll up the streets after me, so I can't be found. No, Daddy, no. She never had a kind word for my playing. Even when I was starting to blow up. She never even let me touch her precious sax.

MOTHER

Thelonious never spent more than fifteen minutes talking to his son about music. I think his boy ended up playing drums. Well, at least my daughter is still playing sax, like me. Just not the right one.

> *MOTHER moves STAGE LEFT. MOTHER puts sax in its case and wraps it.*

DAUGHTER

When is the funeral? Daddy, don't wait on me. I got nothing to say for her. Hunh-uh, Daddy. She threw me out when I quit college. I'm too busy. Especially right now. I'll come home to see you when I can. Just put her to rest.

> *KNOCK at DOOR.*

DAUGHTER

Hold on. The door. It's somebody from the front desk bringing me a package.

> *DAUGHTER opens the door and picks up the package. DAUGHTER unwraps it. Then opens the case.*

DAUGHTER

Oh, Momma.

> *DAUGHTER sits on bed and holds sax. MOTHER rushes back on STAGE and stands behind DAUGHTER. DAUGHTER PLAYS "UNFORGETTABLE." MOTHER embraces DAUGHTER.*

THE END

Birds in Flight

Geese hurtle over rowers in full stroke, themselves hurtling over the Delaware. Such a flock would blot out the sun if it showed its face. The fog on this New Jersey afternoon is more photographic god than weather, declaring sepia the color of everything it touches. Cars jump fog bank to fog bank like flying fish escaping a predator. These birds must be lost, not heading south, but west ahead of the ice rolling in from the Atlantic, the Ancient Mariner in search of another bird to kill and deify.

When I was ten, a boy whose face memory refuses to grant features drug me to a forbidden portion of town to see a white kid he claimed was a friend. When the *friend* came to the door with a shotgun thrown over his shoulder like firewood, I had my doubts.

We ventured to a field cradled with low-hanging fog where the kid took aim at the last streamlined V of geese fleeing winter's early touch. The blast broke the air like a promise. One of the birds faltered as if struck, then plunged to the ground like a crabapple shaken from a tree. The other birds continued their exodus. This is a knowing of sorts. There is no such thing as Promised Land.

Today, I am the only patron in a stylish Indian restaurant. Upturned crystalline glasses reflect light from a gaudy chandelier. The owner has not noticed me. He listens to a language CD that promises to make him an American citizen in twenty lessons or less. I admit I cannot answer half the questions he also gets wrong. Perhaps neither of us belongs in this city, this country of doubt.

When he seats me and asks where I am from, I start by saying that this misty day has left me the courage to answer this question truthfully for the first time. But before I can say more, he laughs as if I have spoken one of those American idioms that he should know but hasn't yet found on his CD. I choose not to pursue it.

As I pay my bill, stuffing a few napkins into my pocket to wipe the fog off my windshield, he asks me how I found his place. I want to tell him I'm trying to find my direction. That I have memories and goals that won't resolve into a plan. That sometimes lost is the only face we own. That his restaurant was the first I encountered that didn't serve goose. But by the time I find my tongue, a woman and her child have opened the door behind me. And the fog tugs on my scarf. It knows my name. It calls me into the only home I know.

A Dream ~~Deferred~~/~~Detained~~ Dismissed

Genealogy

The picture on my computer
is of an ink-grained bird roosting
a dead branch above the tableau.

A slave's foot seeps into blue sludge
so rancid, even buzzards stay clear.
A six-year deathwatch starts its chime.

Look up *crow* and you find *raven*,
rook, jackdaw, vigil seekers:
Everything dies here, even dreams.

Indigo dye is wild theatrics,
vein-deep in skin and ground—
let's call it a bone plague:

Did blood diamonds ever plow
through ancestry like this scythe
through a dozen photo albums?

A queen's beauty has its price:
Slaves perishing for cobalt silk,
racked coughs on hues that split

skin and tumor flesh.   So . . .
I have an ancestor whose feet
& hands pounded pulp for hours

before shrinking and rotting off,
nesting like a bruised tomato
in the crook of my family tree.

Lucia was ripe—sixteen years. Dragging
indigo plants to South Carolina,
tossing death in the Highlands

like a carcass across the floor
of my children's lives. It's all so
noble in print. Where's the whip

slicing the backs red? A cry
like an ugly cough I own
and pass down to them.

Guardians

Grandpa Daniel was in his late seventies. Yet still spry enough to climb the tree in our backyard for figs. He insisted that the only man ever born worth his salt was Martin Luther King Jr.

"I'd take a bullet for that man, yes I would," he said, raining figs down upon his grandson Michael, who raced around the tree beneath his grandpa's scrawny legs poking out of Bermuda shorts. Michael balanced a large wicker basket on his head, always a foot away from where the figs hit.

When they shot the Reverend King, Grandpa Daniel was true to his word. He lay down on his bed, deciding this was the bullet meant for him.

"Soon," he told his daughter-in-law, Caroline, "the good Reverend will wake up, and I will be a hero." But days later, Grandpa Daniel was still alive, and the Reverend was still very much dead. No less true to his word than he was before the announcement of the funeral, Grandpa decided that God hadn't switched him and the Reverend because Grandpa hadn't proven how serious he was. So, Daniel, who had survived seven sit-ins, six police dog attacks, and four hosing downs with water he claimed was colder than Alaskan ice, dug a shallow grave in the backyard. He donned his second-best dress suit—his best, he reasoned, he would wear at his funeral—and lay down in the grave.

That night, it rained. Caroline, who had promised her late husband that she would look after his dad, put an umbrella over the head of the ditch. From his bedroom window, Michael could see his grandpa's feet sticking out from under his grey half-dome of a promise, his wool pants sticking to his legs.

On the day of the funeral, Caroline turned the volume of the old Zenith up loud enough to shake the windows. Really, she was turning it up loud enough to wake the not dead. After a few minutes, the screen door creaked open, and Grandpa shuffled in. His back was caked with mud, but Caroline didn't complain when he sat down on the couch between her and Michael.

When they showed a close-up of King's face, still as dead as Grandpa was not, Daniel took first Michael's hand and then Caroline's. He was crying. "I'm sorry," he said. "I'm sorry. I did everything I could." But he wasn't talking to his grandson. Or his daughter-in-law. He was looking at the TV. He was apologizing to everyone inside the glass.

Fermi Paradox for Black Nerds

Mike says:

"There are 3 Billion Bitches on the Big Blue.
   Some of them too old to fuck.
              (Or too young of course,   Nigga, please)

   But a lot of them probably into black dudes,
                           Big Hair   Big Dicks.
         Even if said dudes ain't
                    DOWN, *ain't hip   ain't happening.*

   And, since we only two busses
   one transfer from any part of town
This ONE party,
         This one night . . ."

   Aside: He's not saying guaranteed Big Bang
                    More like   *Punch-Drunk-Second-Base*
Behind-the-Chicken-Shack   feel-up.

"Hey,
It's a Big Damn Sky tonight.   And a black star is gotta SHINE

somewhere.
Let it be
one of us."

Happiness

"I never complained."
—Woman testifying after twelve years of spousal abuse

I ripped the throat out the possum
before your leash could choke me up.
My tail, the pretty girl beating the drum.
I've got no problem with teeth marks
on the small of my back.

I'm your four-legged Hellraiser.
I've got a pre-broken smile.
I pissed the geranium cause I know
you hate that. I hump your leg.
I love how you beat me
when you're mad.

The Wandering Jew Drunk Dials God

Listen up: I'm on a bus with sixteen nuns
    and a hash pipe. Goose-down fedora with a pimp stick.
    Something's gonna go down between me and the Superior
    unless you acquiesce to a few thangs.   Something nasty.

I've stapled my demands to an altar of dead pigeons.
    Yeah, I knew your son. I called him punk-ass for crying
    on the cross like a momma's boy. You got all pissy, glued
    a pair of eternities to my feet   like the first Jordans.

    (Ahem):
I want a handwritten, "I'm sorry I did you wrong."
    I want *Firefly* back on TV. I want to die.
    I want to come to heaven—
    Just fucking with you. I like this monkey planet.
    I called to see if you were asleep. Or maybe awake, jacking off.

The Party Crashers of Paradise

We bum-rushed the stage,
        this gig in Butte County.
Advertised our arrival with a panicked deer
chewing off a singed hoof.
        A scorched tabby in a birdbath.
        Pinecones
                erupting like roman candles.

Come sunrise,
a hundred flaming fan
                                dancers open
        for us, take the town like fire-
fruit dropped in hell.
A blackout
        curtain is tossed over the sun.

Our drummer went High-Hat
        on some propane tanks
and it all got real.
        Nothing squeals
like
                baby hawks
roasting in a nest.

A sizzling microbus
      humps a Mercedes
           behind a burning bush.
    It's Paradise.
Shit like that happens.

Our frontman scats embers
over the middle school,
      meteors   cratering
      sand through the blind eye
      of monkey bars.

      Sizzling Blue Plate Special:
      burrowing owls
baked Luau style.
      Tree squirrels, fricasseed.
A grandmother
      A brother
A son and daughter
         Two for one'd.

We torched
             EVERYTHING . . .

Except the Starbucks.
We know sacred altars
when we see them,
      the jealous gods of WiFi.

After seventeen days
the Fire Marshall closes the show.
    I can still hear
the whole damn town
        screaming
           OUR NAME.

    It sounds a lot like

        Encore.

Exiled to America

For Daniel Schoorl

Everything
on the *River*
of Painted Birds

remembers his touch.
The muted charcoals.
Dulled pastels layered

on canvas: *la Callejera*
succumbs to *el Malevo*.
Everything not nailed

down swoons.
He's absent
the evasive hue

that erases exile;
the brushstroke
that unwashes *Saudade*.

To watch Daniel set
   his brow, wrangle crimson
   across white, you'd think

he could tease
   a *berretin* to silence,
   honey-walk it into a cage.

But we know
   what he can't see.
   He'll never paint

his mother back
   to an Uruguay street-
   light, swaying to *Por*

una Cabeza beneath
   a pauper's moon, safe
   in his father's arms.

Oppenheimer's Badass Cat

"Most Americans care more about their pets than foreigners."

Hip-Cat Is NOT dead.

He learned   *scammed sham*   from possums.

He's quick-twitch atomic. Shaking thunder-

dust from curtains of clouds, tomcatting nine lives

dusk 'til dawn.

A fur-balled neutrino

jumping ship morality-to-morality

back and forth, couch to table. (But, that was YES-

terday's Blast News.)

Today, he belled the Japanese mailman

then killed him.

Ressurected him from flash-burn negatives

propped him up bulls-eye style   killed him again.

Yeah, you dig it.

    Hip-Cat is Judas-faced

        Robert's master   Julius's slave.

           Riding sideboards   Machine Gun Kelly style

on the Enola Gay.

            Quixotic as shit   an enigma

slapping a *first-ever* High-Five paw

               on the pulse of this New Age.

Yeah . . .   he's his own zeitgeist

            bombed-out irises jiggling.

When Hiroshima
        coughed a lung to heaven

              like a fiery hairball,

    Hip-Cat sneezed   *Nagasaki!*

Then plopped down on the carpet

        to steal a nap.

Rumor is

        Somebody

                threw him a parade.

Joshua in the New World

In that one movie, a fallen angel
    squatted like a vulture on its branch.
    I read a book where a demon's nose
sprouted from its bark and screamed gibberish.

Joshua pushes hands to heaven for water
    stapled to the sky like moths on a screen.
    A new Bible calls for fresh followers, years
(and miles) from that old propheted land.

Wikipedia says the *Utah War* had no
    memorable battles. Mormons didn't
    give the tree its name. Joshua
is a bastardization of Jehoshua.

Yucca trees brand these arid plains,
    bleeding moisture from the dust.
    Their hands claw eyes for prayers
from another continent & desert.

It's untrue: Moses never reached
    Nevada. His staff never parted
    the Sands. Joshua collapsed under
fluorescent lights in a Reno bathroom.

Two bouncers muscled him out a service
    door, hustled past a passed-out Elvis
    and a homeless Jesus. Both of them
one lucky seven throw away from New Canaan.

Frac/Tured

It starts with red smoke acrylic, a floundering desire
to pull the plane out of the first tower like a finger

from a plum. Horsehair, heavy enough to brush
doubt into America, unmans each cockpit. If we

obscure the debris falling top left of the canvas,
we will never know deceit is our kissing cousin.

Pivot the easel. The first tower still crumbles,
but the second plays dodgeball and crouches.

Narratives don't always belong to history's victors.
A swollen flag dances Red & Blue across white sands.

When the painter's brush heals smoke-tinged glass,
one last someone still loses their grip and leaps

from a window. If this is loss of innocence, what
do we tell the Blacks and Indians? Is there another

layer to this tableau, painted over in patriotic greys,
depending on pressure to make us all whole again?

A pale explosion rolls across the green-grey sky.
No. It's a porcupine jutting quills of smoke and fire.

The second plane enters stage left of canvas. An aria
of witness coming face-to-face with its banshee scream.

Finder of Lost Sheep

For Michael Llewellyn's photography workshop for veterans

Do they know your camera cutting

      through saw grass has got their back
      more than a rifle or machete ever will?

Most vets are stateside when

      the domino—once fallen—jumps back
      upright, roll-calling them back to a minefield.

Something as simple as a sparkler

      tossed across a manicured lawn on the fourth
      blasts a tunnel open to a sallow field in Vietnam.

Michael can't know if fingers that

      balanced trip wires on a blade of grass
      can set shutters fast enough to fill

a hole in memories and lost sunsets.

But, dammit, somebody's got to teach
these survivors the difference between

a rifle barrel and a child's arm.

The dull copper scent of VA bunks scatters
reason like a hornet's nest dragged across cement.

Past-due mortgage bills roll up

to mortar tubes. When the smoke clears,
there's Michael hauling a hurdy-gurdy

of flags into focus like butterfly

wings pinned to cork and balsa wood.
Someone opens a cave in a pantry door.

A sniper's bullet rises like quail

from a field. A point-man pours, then repours
the same cup of gasoline on his head,

setting decades ablaze. It's always

the leaden crevices that nest the most fears.
Where the camera flash needs to dig deepest.

A sergeant's silhouette ghosts

    across a polished lens. Then scurries back
    into the underbrush. These soldiers hopped

a broom with the devil.

    Now they struggle with stillness
    as a flashlight sets the focal point

on the back of their irises,

    pulling at whatever secrets the mind
    stashed away in rusted footlockers.

If our loved ones' days end

    with a lynchpin blowing their mind
    to smithereens, aren't we all doomed?

Cue Michael, huddled

    over a tripod like the last Lord of Regret,
    trying to drag a kill shot back into a barrel.

Woods to Grow Out Of

I've learned the word *Exactly*
    and it fits me like the hymn
    my body calls its church
        every day school is out.

I like summer for its secrets
    The red clay of the South
        How the word **South**
Gets a capital **S** and means:

    Some roads are forbidden
    Some neighborhoods foreboden
    Some words forgotten
    Some eyes foreclosed by gun or rope.

These words mean nothing and everything   *Exactly*
        similar or sense-making.

There's a promise of   *happenings*
    painful but no one talks about
        winter in Indian Summer.

        Yet everyone knows:

My brother says black *means   not so okay to the world*
My uncle says Parliament will come to reclaim the pyramids
My grandfather says nothing to me I ever hear just right
Grandmama *says* Jesus *and everyone grumbles* Amen.

But,   isn't there *always a something*
                    no one ever says to their children?
Until shoeless boys like me grow dizzy with thoughts
                they can't pin a word to   or
                    put a finger in?

Everyone in the world never talks
                    about me   to me
        and that's FINE.

        Today   SUMMER runs
        like a puppy
            chasing butterflies

        a divining rod spinning forever nowhere
                        Exactly:

That janitor who worked twenty years
in the white school got foolish bought
a home in their neighborhood and got
his house not himself blown up dead.

I hear houses complain about the heat all the time.

Especially when summer swings from their clogged
                gutters like a grinning chimp.

I have named   these woods
    Five Boxed Corners of Fruit
                for the grapes, figs, apples,
   strawberries, blackberries
        and snake berries we don't eat. *Six.*

Tomorrow,
        I'll scale the tall hill past
   creek moat
        past the sunken mine shaft
    and be free

Even if there are   ticks with their blood bags
                they stuff like Santa Claus
Even if there are   black widows with hourglasses
                leaking the Days of Our Lives

    Even if the world ends
      over the peak of the next hill
        Ends with animals

carrying crazy big teeth. I'll let them
    bite me   a little
      long as they   snuggle up
        and tell me
            their secrets.

Red and Yellow Quartet

A pub table in a kitchen at an upscale Harlem Renaissance jazz club. BOSSMAN and LEON, light-skinned Negro musicians, toast their completed set. Kitchen noises. Applause from offstage. "Let's hear it one more time for the Red and Yellow Quartet!"

BOSSMAN

We tore the doors off this place tonight.

LEON

Best damn music these white folks ever seen!

BOSSMAN

You was right. That NEW GUY handles his sticks. Where you find him?

LEON

Heard about he and his brother doing a set in Charlene's off Lenox Avenue. For chump change.

BOSSMAN

Fresh off the bus?

LEON

Some backwater Mississippi town. He still sleeping in a flop house.

BOSSMAN

We'll keep NEW GUY, but his brother . . . Where they at?

LEON

Talking in the alley. What you gon' tell NEW GUY?

BOSSMAN

I got this. Already talked to his brother.

NEW GUY enters kitchen from alley. He is angry.

NEW GUY
We need to talk.

BOSSMAN
Slow yourself, now.

LEON
Calm down. Have a drink.

NEW GUY
Fuck you.

BOSSMAN
Keep your voice down. Can't have the management see us causing a fuss.

NEW GUY
The same management that's got you eating in the kitchen?

LEON
Where you expect we'd be eatin'? Out there with the white folks?

BOSSMAN
Boy, just sit yourself for a minute. C'mon now.

NEW GUY does not sit. Glowers at BOSSMAN.

BOSSMAN
From that look on your puss, I guess you talked to your brother.

NEW GUY
You don't like the way we play, you should man up and say something to me instead of my little brother.

LEON
You play just fine.

BOSSMAN
Mighty fine.

NEW GUY
Then why the hell are we fired?

> *BOSSMAN's name is called offstage to rising APPLAUSE.*

BOSSMAN
Let me go check on that. LEON, fill him in.

> *BOSSMAN exits.*

LEON
Sit down.

NEW GUY
We did good out there.

LEON
You ain't fired.

NEW GUY
That's not what my brother said.

LEON
You know what. If your ass is too good to sit and hear what I have to say, then maybe we can't work together no how.

> *NEW GUY sits, but not quite up to the table.*

LEON
Good. Now have a drink.

NEW GUY
I ain't thirsty.

LEON

The first one comes out of your pay, so you might as well drink it.

NEW GUY

I didn't agree to nothing like that.

LEON

And your dinner.

NEW GUY

You two a bunch of damn crooks.

LEON *(laughing)*

You think it's us? Open your eyes, fool. What part of this place screams "Negro heaven" to you? That broom closet they give us to change in? I saw your face when you saw what color the crowd was.

NEW GUY

This ain't no different from Mississippi.

LEON

Yeah, it is. It just ain't as different as you thought it might be.

NEW GUY

This is the black part of town.

> *BOSSMAN enters stage. LOUD applause.*

LEON

But this here club ain't black, is it?

BOSSMAN

And your brother is.

NEW GUY

What the fuck you mean?

LEON

We hadn't gotten that far, yet.

BOSSMAN

Well, let's speed this shit up. (To NEW GUY) What's the name of our little troupe?

NEW GUY

Red and Yellow Quartet.

LEON

Folks with money . . .

BOSSMAN

White folks he means.

LEON

White folks tend to prefer their entertainment . . .

BOSSMAN

Their colored entertainment to be closer to their own shade.

NEW GUY

What?

LEON

They prefer their coffee with a little cream.

NEW GUY

So, the reason my brother is in the alley pissed off . . .

BOSSMAN

Is because you ain't in Kansas no more, Dorothy.

> *BOSSMAN's name is called offstage. More applause.*

LEON

Tonight, we was in a pinch. Lost two of our players. So I hired you, kind of figuring you and your brother looked alike.

BOSSMAN

Listen, they calling for us to be introduced as the new house band. The manager ain't interested in your brother. But, you got a spot if you want it. Make your decision.

NEW GUY

If he don't play, I don't play.

BOSSMAN and LEON stand.

BOSSMAN

That's your call. You can toe this line or the bread line.

LEON

Lots of musicians in Harlem. Just sayin'.

BOSSMAN

I'll give you a few seconds to join us. Otherwise . . .

BOSSMAN and LEON exit stage toward dining area.
LOUD APPLAUSE. After a few seconds, NEW GUY looks
both ways and stands.

We the *(Chameleon)* People

Unjumping the Broom

Our bedroom   is a circus, moths
        hang from trapezes.

Doubts   are the lions
        jumping
        through hoops and garters,
                setting curtains aflame.

You say the broken

        fork in the sink   was an omen.
                Clown paper scales
the walls of your sleep.

        The face paint coating my dreams
                can't mask our problems.

No matter.
        Nothing's
                random. I'm dragging
        a foot through cotton candy,

trolling for good news.   Something
to get me
          out of bed. You slip on a nightgown

          dotted with crickets.
          They chirp for the moon's spotlight

traipsing through our open window
          on
                    camel-stilt
                              beams.

          Our anemic slice
          of wedding cake   is missing
                              from the freezer.

Tossed center ring
for the elephants to trample.

          I blame the hyena
                    or the media.

Anyone except
          that silhouetted, pissed
          off YOU
                    holding the plastic gun

with the paper BANG!-
                    flag
        aimed at my temple.

I've gone deaf from its repeated

                Silence.

I know . . .
                tomorrow night, let's drag
        the cannon bedside.
One of us climbs in.

The other   dons the clown car
        like a cheap suit
and starts   RUNNING.

Let's see
        who gets the Hell out
        of this marriage   *faster.*

Easter Morning Prayer

Better than being Born:

       If you knew I hitched a ride

               every time

          kissing your neck,

   you'd love turning your back on me.

I am imagining   happy face stickers

           on your ass,

               because   I love your ass.

And the smiles go up & down

         down-up   and-down as you walk.

Better than Resurrection:

        My laughter during sex

      is me smiling out loud.

You don't notice

        the lightning bolt I imagine

               on your forehead that pulses

           faster   fastest

    when I

        (quite the favorite student)

   do something brilliant.

That bolt   insane jolt   and lightning
                                    slays me.

Until all I can think
is how dying for your wide-eyed

                    Joker-Smile is the best religion.

                    Better even than Death.

Hunter's Moon

Hunters hunt. Dan and his boy draw the same
thin lie across the sheriff's desk. Their closed
gums smug. Guns snug—the traditional pose,
tucked under armpits to keep them silent.
The Toyota's bed is slick, a dripping redness
the hollowed-out deer, reed thin, is too small
to alibi. The sheriff walks heavy-footed through
their hunters' tale: they were shooting tree
rats. A bullet of theirs spots, stops a deer's heart.

It's near dawn. But star-shine still pierces the mist
like a rapier. He counts and recounts their words,
until sleep peels doubt off the linoleum. Moonlight
can't unearth the lynched child's corpse. And he
can't shake the swamp gas sag from their story.
It's a trap, this slow drawl, part of this old South.
The last ingredient in the miasma, the hunter's
wife calls, begging her men home before sun-up.

The Saint of McClatchy Park

Baptized in knowing. The birth waters never quite retreated from his mind's hollows. His loping stroll past skateboarders *Be careful Oh-Oh* because that's the kind of child he is. Autism clutches his brain, three sections of Thomas cradled like a wounded bird to his chest. It's stately. His stare hovers, scanning left-right, a hummingbird granting benediction to sun and wind-shine. We should all be blessed with such farseeing: forgiving sickness in bare patches of grass, sand & mulch escaping fenced-in guardrails. Careful-shoed summer tiptoes past picnic tables, abandoned scooters. He lies over the drain beneath the giant-headed turtle spraying cool relief, careful—Oh, so careful—shielding Thomas from the sewer grate's slivered mouth to the river streams.

Lost tumblings of leaves slip brown&green to the concrete. How to explain: There is fog caressing a brilliance untapped. A geyser of knowledge straining against a rock mantle. Be patient. Cap your despair and prayer. Bless the thickness sloshing, because, doesn't everyone deserve a poem? He mumbles "Happy Together" to Thomas, the last song he heard. Sprinklers bend over the scene. A rainbow caps his skull like a bridge to everywhere. One child laughs. His father snatches her collar back from this hazardous calling of ugly roads.

I take little notice. I'm busy genuflecting, knelt in beauteous supplication. Heat rambles across the pavement like a host of buffalo reclaiming ghost plains of memory. It hurts, honestly, knowing he might understand all he can't explain. At times, sudden fits rage, embrace this hard body growing so fast. Sometimes he looks at me and I almost swoon to the rapid dawning of saintliness in his crooked smile.

Veterans of Foreign Wars

Driving a street whose name
      is lost to this crippling narrative,
            I spot my brother stumbling

hot-spit gravel
      drunk on another Sacramento
            heatwave. Lost in the needle

song I was too stupid too soft
      too *something* to protect him from.
            Don't blame me. It was my car that

hopped two yellow lines in an angry crescent,
      switching lanes like channels, like a dog
            rushing to heel at the feet of a lost master.

Temples of dust rose from the ditch.
      I flung the door open, my heart wedged
            beneath my seatbelt, fluttering like a fat

moth in my chest. Was I Ahab
    or the whale? The iron-sharp
        harpoon or the pale giant's triumph?

Either stifling heat or grief baked
    my mind simple. Yes, this man's
        Pompei-flaked skin and helpless grin

are the same as the brother
    I knew, trapped in a body ravaged
        by mortar blast, a prison where all the keys

are swallowed by angry Gods.
    But I lost that brother two decades
        and an Iraqi leap away. This stranger's wariness

says all you need to know
    about the silence between that afternoon
        and me those last seconds; a sparrow dead

on its perch. His shoulder
    brushed my bumper as he listed
        through a fresh wave of dust devils.

What he mumbles
    at my closing door before
        tilting away, I will never know.

But I believe it was *I love you.*
    As my car dug out of the ditch,
        I swear to you   *that's* what he said.

How We Got Here from There

Dedicated to your struggle, whatever it may be.

I cross-swam
a river snake-bit.
Coolness pounded

into my temples.
A requiem of angels
took pity, dipped

one wing, dusted
off my knees, blessed
my skin. Barefoot

I haunted back-
roads, shouldering
your memory:

Sober-eyed &
mysterious. Howled
a pregnant moon

down from a willow
tree. Cracked bone-
lust and sucked

marrow. Hexed
my guilted shadow.
Somersaulted naked

through poppy fields.
Licked dew off the
back of headstones.

For six months
I dodged poison
darts. Took a sledge

to the chest,
collapsed. Caught
your scent on a breeze.

Rose like Christ,
a punch-drunk flagbearer,
ears genuine & swollen.

Enabled by your name, I
Stumbled over fireflies.
Sharpened my canines.

Yanked myself forward.
Brushed off my heart.
Put it back in my chest.

Set my head skyward
looking for a sign.
Your face in the clouds.

Blackberries

Side by side, we walked this last dirt road together. "It's a star-catcher moon," my brother said. "See how it's shaped like an upside-down sickle. Like a cupped hand. See what I mean?"

He was pointing with his left hand because his right arm was broken, thudding against his side like a screen door in a breeze. His left hand wasn't much better; bloody, the fingers swollen, but at least it worked. He held the hand to the sky, cupped it beneath the moon.

"See? You could drop a star right into it."

He was home from Yale for all of three days, but you wouldn't know it from the way he looked. There was no Ivy League in that swollen jaw or black eye. Ivy League students didn't hang out on unlit, shit-kicking dust roads with fucked up little brothers like me. My vision swam sideways and then rushed back, slamming against my eyes, wobbling them in their sockets. My right knee lost focus and buckled under the clouding sky.

He was having trouble keeping up with me. His breath wheezed like a tractor that had pulled one too many plows. As if one lung wasn't working so good. Still, he wouldn't shut up.

"That star above the moon. I know it looks like it's standing still, but it's falling. Almost too slow to see, but it's falling, I tell you. If you watch it long enough, you'll see it drop right into the moon."

At twelve, squeezed into the tire swing in the backyard while he sat on the porch telling me stories, I might have believed this crap. But that boy was gone, buried beneath five summers of drought and withered tobacco harvests.

"It's Mars," I said. I was guessing. I couldn't look up to check. My neck was full of ground glass. My star-gazing days were over for a little while. Maybe longer.

We were on the downside of a grade. The road rose to a steep crest behind us. There were no headlights coming over the hill. Not yet. We shuffled along while the crickets mocked us from the blackberry bushes.

I thought I heard a truck three times before it was real, a diesel engine building up its chops. I spun all the way around and faced the hill. I hoped my brother would keep walking, prayed he would. He turned and stood beside me. Headlights climbed the backside of the hill like a forest fire.

"I don't need you to fight my battles for me," I said.

"I know."

"I didn't even ask you to come back." He put his hand on my shoulder. I shrugged it off.

The truck straddled the top of the hill like a rabid animal, crazed eyes tunneling through the dark. It paused, sighted us, then leaped into its charge. Sirens went off in my head. We moved like the brothers time and distance had made us, diving to opposite sides of the road. Thorns tore at me like every thought I'd had of him since he left me to rot on the farm.

The pickup spun dirt, then roared to a stop. Boots hit the ground. I stumbled through the briar for hours or minutes, moonlight tracking me like a hell hound. I fell into a clearing where a farmhouse squatted, dressed up in faded reds, peeling whites. I got to my knees and took off for the safety of the welcome mat I hoped was on the porch. It was close. Tantalizingly close.

The breath on my neck told me I wouldn't make it.

Maisey Gets a Washing Machine

Her mother—sleeping in rags stitched
from curtains too worn for the parlor,
singed by candles—was raped
by an uncle who swears old rye, no
glass no ice, deafened him to her screams.
The child born is named for a bird too
stupidly lazy to hatch her own eggs.
But this Maisey is a pro. By twenty
she's bred two to a burly, towheaded
man whose fingertips fit the small
of her back like a skeleton key.

Let me lay it down for you: her man
splits for a less dingy horizon. Hoisting
three jobs like kindling, every hour
feels like scraping crumbs off toast
too burned to eat. The dream: a brand-new
washing machine, all the works. A silver
and chrome suit of armor to stand guard
between the kitchen and the back door.

Slick advertisements and a slicker banker
convince her payments will be easier

than saving. One job sinks into quick-
sand. Another sheds her like an old shoe.

The steam-pressed young man prowling
Saturday morning housewives sneers
when she says she hasn't had time
to think about elections. She brains him
with his clipboard. The judge can't relate.
At least when her children visit her jail cell,
their clothes are cleaner than starched sunshine.

Pretty Boy Sanchez

Legend has it:

Sanchez's right cross whistled like a train
through a tunnel. He had a hotline to Satan,
dropping hellfire into his hook. His left thigh
carved from petrified oak, the right Gibraltar.
His mother chewed gunpowder instead
of sorghum. His father gifted his son those
quick-twitch ballet feet before every fight.

When he went down in the fifth to a Jersey
pipefitter paler than blind-fish, Mexican
fans stormed the ring. They couldn't touch
the gringo, so they lynched Pretty Boy.

Some called it a mistake. Some said there
was a kind of blindfold in their bloodlust.
Years later, a *sabia* schooled that leeching
his veins was the only way to get back
the song he borrowed from his people.

American Bataan

Hot concrete beckons the raccoon
until it scutters across the driveway
in broad daylight, surely rabid,
unconcerned with death or afterlife   or
the cat he mauled in the brambles across
the street   or the dog that tore his ear
into a crimson rag flopping over one eye.

        The Dodge Dart's grill is littered with bugs.
        Wooden blocks for tires, a tarnished grill,
        and slanted smile. Skinny tomatoes staked
        to a dying garden glisten beneath sprinklers.

His eyes are fixed on a fake horizon, flaking
skyline of the neighbor's wooden fence.
In the next yard, an aging Doberman is waiting
under a fruitless Japanese myrtle, spoiling
for a fight, a reblossoming of past glories.

        In the house, the owner eats, as if it is his idea,
        ramen three times a day. Even the canned
        beets wait in triage, soldiers knowing the next

scalpel is for them. Tapered candles in mason
jars dot the inner landscape like mute, accusatory
children, awaiting nightfall, awaiting usefulness.

The raccoon, his fur molting in clumps, every
drop of water a hot swelling in his throat, stares
at the tomatoes, then the man in the window.
A thickness worms through both their eyes.
His grin tells the man he knows, he feels
there is respite over the next fence for both
of them if they can find the strength to climb.

Lost in the World Machine

I'm 17&Black, nimble as Jack, jumping I-beams like candles.
An air hose hisses like Medusa's head tied to my wrist.
This Refining Machine performs the alchemy to turn
rusted steel virginal again. But it's stinging me to death.
Grey-hot pellets jet from tiny holes; blackstrap horseflies
cutting away the oxidation. Like the foreman's gaze,
they always find the tender flesh. I'm summer college

> fodder, working shit jobs before humping
> a train back to Raleigh. The welders' first
> sparks of the day always make me flinch.
> Dust-laden smoke circles the rafters, ropy
> chains hanging like man-o-war tendrils,
> like a trembling curtain of almost lynchings.

I'm a harlequin playing cards with somebody else's
deck: I know as much about refining steel as I do about
studying textbooks. I'm hard-tracked to do both or neither
until pressure geysers out my brain, until I roll snake
eyes with the future. Maybe—if I threw myself into
this machine, I could save my feet this tortured road.

Crosstown bus passes dig deep into minimum
wage. An old lady shuffles after my bus as it pulls
from the curb. I don't reach the pull cord in time
to give her a fighting chance. Or, like my absentee
father might say, maybe I just didn't try hard enough.

Catching a Cotton Ball

> *LUCAS and BEATRICE in a car. BEATRICE is driving. LUCAS is looking at a newspaper. Something is wrong with his hands. He struggles to turn a page. BEATRICE takes one hand off the wheel and turns it for him. BEATRICE is clearly irritated by him and with him.*

LUCAS
Look here. Hoover is going to put a tax on gasoline. As if times ain't bad enough.

> *BEATRICE says nothing.*

LUCAS
Just goes to show. Was the right time to leave Texas.

> *LUCAS tosses the newspaper in the back, unfolded. He picks up a map from the floorboard at his feet.*

LUCAS
Just like I said. Timing! And you always acting like I don't know nothing right.

> *LUCAS finds something he likes, then holds the map up to BEATRICE. She fends it off.*

LUCAS
Just look at it.

BEATRICE
I'm driving.

LUCAS

Then pull over.

> *BEATRICE keeps driving.*

LUCAS

Pull over up here.

> *BEATRICE keeps driving. LUCAS starts to say something, then stops. They drive in silence. LUCAS notices something approaching.*

LUCAS

That a caravan? Negroes moving into Texas. *(Laughs)* Ain't nothing back there for them. Pull over, let's talk to them.

> *BEATRICE speeds up.*

LUCAS

Bee. The road . . . Bee . . . Pull over!

> *BEATRICE yanks the wheel to the left.*

LUCAS

Don't ditch us in the cotton, Woman!

> *Car stops abruptly. A procession of cars is getting closer. LUCAS waves.*

LUCAS

Howdy! Yeah. Yeah.

> *While LUCAS talks, BEATRICE gets out of the car. Grabs a bag from the back and sprints out into the cotton. She finds a hiding place and squats down. She is calm in the cotton.*

LUCAS

Just keep heading down this way. Twenty-three miles. Then a left at the
fork. Yeah. Naw. We came from New York first. Then spent some time
picking here. It was good. Weevils ain't got this far yet. We made our
fortune. My wife's cotton farm. We sold it. Heading back to New. Naw.
Ain't no machine ever pick cotton faster than a man. Plenty of jobs, I tell
ya. You just go on. See I'm right. Evening.

> *LUCAS watches the procession pass. He waves.*

BEATRICE

Why you lie to them?

> *LUCAS starts, surprised. He notices the door open and
> BEATRICE gone.*

LUCAS

Woman, where you at?

> *LUCAS fumbles with the door handle, but his hands
> betray him. He gives up and exits the car driver side,
> into the cotton field.*

LUCAS

Bee, come on out of the cotton.

BEATRICE

Ain't nothin' but starvation waiting on those folks.

> *LUCAS walks around, looking for BEATRICE. They are
> engaged in an intricate dance. BEATRICE easing through
> the cotton, low, almost dancing, avoiding LUCAS easily.
> LUCAS struggling through, being scraped, unable to see
> BEATRICE. The cotton is too high. It does not like him.*

LUCAS

All I did was give them some hope.

BEATRICE

Evil. That's all you is. Selfish and evil.

LUCAS

Come on now. Stop this foolishness. Let's get back on the road.

BEATRICE

Sold my momma's place. For what? That little bit of scratch.

LUCAS

This was a good move for us. We made out. Stop this, Bee! Come on out.

BEATRICE

Blood money. That house been in my family for three generations. Now, white folks own my momma's grave. Her bones. You said we was gon' work that farm. Raise a family there.

LUCAS

That ain't fair. We tried. What we know about cotton? We was gon' lose that place and you know it. Big farmers. Tractors. More labor than us. All that. That such things.

BEATRICE

You swore we was gon' send some money to help my sister in Mobile. You swore!

LUCAS

There wasn't never enough to send. How come I can't tell where you at?

BEATRICE

The cotton knows, Luke. It knows. That's why it took your hands.

LUCAS

Stop with your hoodoo nonsense. Touch of arthritis, is all.

> *BEATRICE picks a cotton ball. She holds her forearms together, hands facing up, and rolls a cotton ball up and down her arms.*

BEATRICE

Cotton remembers me. You can't just show up down here and act like the cotton's supposed to know you, too. With your evil self.

LUCAS

It's getting dark. Bee. Bee! I'm getting mad. When I get my hands on you . . .

BEATRICE *(Chanting)*

Cotton don't like you. I don't like you. Cotton don't like you. I don't like you . . .

LUCAS

I'm going back to the car.

> *LUCAS turns around, lost.*

LUCAS

Which way the car?

> *BEATRICE stands, holds up the bag.*

BEATRICE

You gon' leave without the money?

> *LUCAS swears, stumbles for the spot where BEATRICE was, but she has already pulled the bag down and disappeared into the cotton.*

LUCAS

I'm gon' kill you when I find you.

BEATRICE

Not if the cotton gets you first.

LUCAS

Awww . . . You know I was just playin'. It's getting dark. C'mon. Let's go, honey.

BEATRICE

My mother's farm. Three generations. Gone just like that.

> *LUCAS is getting nervous. He searches frantically through the cotton. The cotton returns his angst. BEATRICE crawls through the cotton to the car. She gets in the car. LUCAS hears the car door shut, but he still can't tell the direction.*

BEATRICE

Cotton took your hands. Now cotton's gonna take the rest of you.

LUCAS

Arthritis! Arthritis! Not no damn cotton. Bee, don't you leave me.

> *BEATRICE leans out of the car and picks a cotton ball. She plays with it, blowing it in the air. LUCAS is crazed. He stumbles, falls.*

LUCAS *(Spitting, pulling cotton fluff from his mouth.)*
Bee! Help me!

> *The cotton ball escapes BEATRICE's hand, slipping out the window.*

BEATRICE *(Laughs)*

Oh, no. You ain't getting away that easy.

> *BEATRICE starts the car, LUCAS choking on cotton fluff and dust.*

LUCAS

For God's sake, Bee!

> *BEATRICE pulls out of the ditch and drives away, chasing the cotton ball.*

Anywhere but Here

Woman   I kissed you twice
yesterday   knowing we will
be dead   before we ever meet
again   That, given salt   our lips
would dive deep for wrecks
in foreign seas.   To hear the
preacher tell it   bruised flesh
is a sin.   But, so is regret.
And some gospel   is cruel.
And some waters   dark.
We will each enjoy the Dead
Sea   floating in its own
spoil of lost loves   refusing
to let anyone   dive deep
enough   to steal its secrets.

BACKWATERS PRIZE IN POETRY

The Backwaters Prize in Poetry was suspended from 2005 to 2011.

To order or obtain more information on these or other University of Nebraska Press titles, visit nebraskapress.unl.edu.